OUR PLANET

Glaciers

LYNNE PATCHETT

Troll Associates

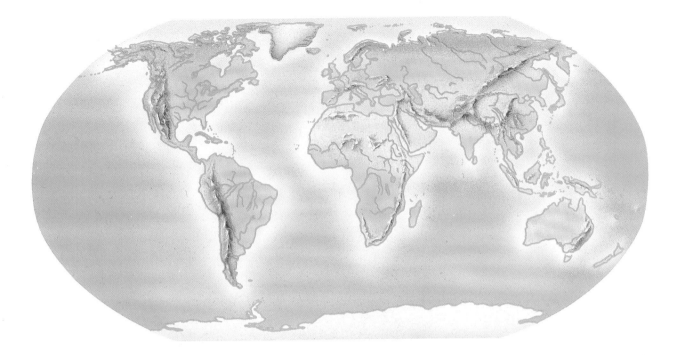

Library of Congress Cataloging-in-Publication Data

Patchett, Lynne.
   Glaciers / by Lynne Patchett ; illustrated by Robert Burns.
      p.   cm. — (Our planet)
      Summary: Describes the formation and movement of different types
of glaciers, their effect on the land, and the animals and plants
that inhabit them.
      ISBN 0-8167-2751-1 (lib. bdg.)   ISBN 0-8167-2752-X (pbk.)
      1. Glaciers—Juvenile literature. [1. Glaciers.] I. Burns,
Robert, ill.   II. Title.   III. Series.
GB2403.8.P38   1993
551.3′1—dc20   91-45080

Published by Troll Associates

Edited by Neil Morris and Kate Woodhouse

Design by Sally Boothroyd

Picture research by Jan Croot

Printed in the United States of America, bound in Mexico.

10 9 8 7 6 5 4 3 2 1

Illustrators
Robert Burns: 13, 16, 19, 29
Martin Camm: 25, 27
Chris Forsey: 14
David McAllister: 23
Mike Roffe: 6-7, 21

Picture credits
GSF Picture Library: 6-7, 8-9, 10, 15, 20, 24,   24-5
Hutchison Library: Richard House: 28
NHPA: Stephen Krasemann: 29
NHPA: John Shaw: 4, 26
John Noble: 18
Survival Anglia: Joel Bennett: 16, 26-27
Survival Anglia: Edwin Mickleburgh: 22
Survival Anglia: Rick Price: 17, 30, 31
Survival Anglia: Colin Willock: 18-19
Tony Waltham: 1, 5, 8, 11, 15, 31
ZEFA: cover, 12-13, 30

Cover photo: La Mer de Glace in the French Alps

Title page: Columbian Icefield in the Canadian
Rockies

CONTENTS

The unseen land of ice

When you look at rocks, mountains, or valleys, you are probably looking at a landscape that was formed by slow-moving, thick sheets of ice, thousands or millions of years ago. Every year, there are new discoveries that convince people that ice covered different parts of Earth at some time in its history. There was ice in Europe, North America, New Zealand, South America, and even the Sahara Desert.

There have been three ice ages in the past 600 million years. The most recent one began about two million years ago. Between 20,000 and 15,000 years ago the average temperature of the world was 11°-16°F (6°-9°C) lower than it is now. New York, London, and Cologne were all buried under ice, much as Antarctica is today.

Earthquakes, volcanoes, and hurricanes all affect the landscape of Earth, but glaciers are more powerful than all of these. Glaciers do not have such an immediate effect, but one that is much longer lasting.

▲ This is how the tiny crystals of ice in snowflakes look when they are magnified. They are complicated and beautiful.

Glaciers are formed when the tiny crystals of ice in snowflakes melt under the pressure of more snow on top of them. The water from these melted crystals freezes into small grains of snow, which then freeze together. This type of snow is called *firn* or *névé*. Gradually all the air is squeezed out and the small grains become *glacier ice*.

▶ The Alaska Range covered with glaciers, ice, and snow down to the *snow line*.

Types of glaciers

There are four main types of glaciers. *Ice caps* or *ice sheets* are very large masses of ice that cover almost all the land features. They are also called *continental glaciers*. They spread down from mountainous areas to lowlands. Today Greenland, Antarctica, and the seas surrounding them are covered by ice caps. Although ice caps take up only one tenth of the land surface, they hold over nine tenths of all the ice on Earth between them!

An *alpine, valley,* or *mountain glacier* begins as a mass of ice in the highlands and moves like a tongue of ice between two mountains. The largest valley glaciers today are in the mountain ranges of the northern Andes, the Rockies, the Himalayas, and the Alps. Many African ranges have large glaciers: the largest are on Mount Kilimanjaro and Mount Kenya.

Piedmont glaciers form when valley glaciers move onto the lowland plains and join together. An example of this is the Malaspina Glacier in Alaska.

Cirque glaciers feed into valley glaciers. They are really small masses of ice that develop in a rock hollow at the head of a valley or on a mountainside. The Matterhorn in the Swiss Alps was shaped by cirque glaciers.

Ice will continue to form at the head of the glacier up in the highlands. The weight of the accumulating ice forces the glacier to move very slowly down the valley, where ice melts at the *snout* at the snow line. This ice loss is called *ablation*. In some years, however, more ice accumulates than is lost through ablation. This makes the glacier thicken and move a little faster.

▶ The Aletsch valley glacier in Switzerland is the longest in Europe. Smaller valley and cirque glaciers feed into it.

alpine, valley, or mountain glacier   piedmont glacier   cirque glacier

How ice moves

Glaciers move at different speeds. It is not necessarily the largest ones that move fastest. Most move about 300 feet (100 meters) a year, mostly in summer. Sometimes they move fast for a short while. One glacier in Iceland was measured as moving 350 feet (107 meters) a day.

▲ Crevasses run with and across the flow of a glacier. They are a danger for mountaineers.

Glaciers combine two forms of movement, called *basal sliding* and *creep*. Basal sliding occurs when a glacier moves over its own bed. It is caused by a freeze-thaw action. Pressure in the ice causes parts of it to break and melt. Although the melted ice refreezes almost immediately, there is just enough time for it to trickle a short distance down the slope. This is similar to what happens when you ice-skate. The friction of the thin skate blades breaks and melts the ice, allowing the blades to glide along the narrow groove of water before it refreezes.

If it is too cold for the ice to melt, the glacier stays frozen to its bed and can only move internally, or creep. Glaciers creep when the ice crystals in the glacier are moved around by the tremendous pressure of the ice. This makes the different layers within the glacier slide, or creep, over one another. Glaciers move more quickly at the surface and in the center than at the sides and bottom. These different rates of movement combined with the internal pressure produce deep cracks, or *crevasses*.

▲ There are several glaciers moving slowly down the side of this mountain. Some of the mountain has not been covered with ice. There is a dark stripe of medial moraine between two of the glaciers on the right.

As the glacier moves downhill, it takes clay, sand, and rocks from the floor and sides of the valley with it. This waste forms a ridge called a *moraine*. When two glaciers flow together, their moraines join and form a dark stripe called a *medial moraine*.

9

Glacial landscapes

As ice moves, it changes the land by eroding, transporting, and depositing it elsewhere. Ice caps scour the land beneath them, rather like a steel-wool pad. But valley glaciers produce more dramatic effects as they work their way down from the highlands.

▼ It is easy to see why U-shaped valleys got their name! This excellent example of a U-shaped valley is in Switzerland.

There are three types of glacial erosion. *Sapping*, or *frost-shattering*, breaks and widens the cracks in rocks by the constant thawing and freezing of ice. When water freezes to become ice, it expands, which would enlarge any crack in the rock. This action forms *cirques*, which are steep-sided dips in the side of a mountain. *Plucking*, or *quarrying*, pulls rocks away from the valley sides as the ice moves over them. *Abrasion* carries rocks along and scours other rocks.

Valley glaciers are formed in valleys already made by rivers at a time when the climate was warmer. Although rivers move up to 100,000 times faster than glaciers, their effect on the landscape is much smaller. After the glacier has melted, many valleys are left U-shaped. The glacier has rounded the bottom of the valley. The Lauterbrunnen Valley in Switzerland is a good example of a U-shaped alpine valley.

Large glaciers are often fed by smaller side glaciers that flow into their upper parts. Large glaciers erode the valleys deeper than the tributaries, so when the glacier eventually melts, these tributaries are left "hanging" on the valley sides. These *hanging valleys* often produce beautiful waterfalls, such as those in the Yosemite Valley in California.

Fjords form when very deep U-shaped valleys eat their way right down to, and sometimes below, sea level. When glaciers melt, the sea level rises and floods the valley. The Nordvest Fjord in Greenland is the longest fjord in the world, measuring 195 miles (313 kilometers).

▲ The Yosemite falls plunge 2,425 feet (740 meters), a fine example of a hanging valley.

The ice ages

Today about one tenth of Earth's surface is covered by ice. At various times in its history, a third of Earth has been covered by ice. Scientists believe that the most recent ice age began about two million years ago, when the climate cooled enough for ice to build up.

The ice sheet that covered North America spread over Canada and beyond the Great Lakes into the United States. Northern Europe and most of Britain were covered by ice. The landscape would have looked much like Antarctica today, where only the peaks of the Trans-antarctic Mountains can be seen above the ice that is over two miles (three kilometers) deep. The sea level was lower, so Asia and North America, Britain and Europe, and Australia and New Guinea were all linked by land.

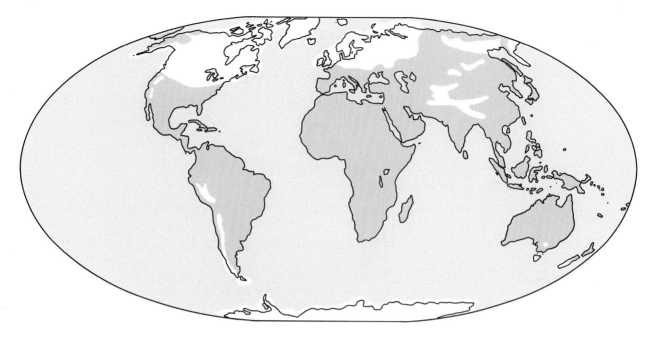

◀ It is difficult to imagine that under the ice of the Antarctic there is land, just as on the continents of Europe and North America. It is impossible to tell what it might look like.

▲ This present-day map shows the areas covered by ice during the last great ice age. Scientists have calculated this from the marks on rocks made by glaciers thousands of years ago.

The weight of the ice sheets was strong enough to depress Earth's crust. Areas of northern Europe and North America have risen since the ice melted, and continue to rise. Large parts of the bases of the Greenland and Antarctic ice caps are at present below sea level.

Between 1450 and 1850 there was the Little Ice Age, when most of the glaciers in the world advanced, and rivers that now never freeze had several inches of ice over them. This change of temperature was very small compared with previous ice ages.

We live in an *interglacial* period, between ice ages.

The evidence of land forms

When the glaciers of the last ice age melted, they deposited rock and other materials in the lowlands. This material produced distinctive land forms, or moraines, that provide scientists with evidence of the glacial movements of the past. The soil in a moraine is rich in nutrients and therefore extremely valuable to farmers.

The land forms are divided into particular types. Boulders transported and left stranded by glaciers are called *erratics*. Some erratics were carried long distances. In East Greenland, for example, there are huge boulders in the middle of the tundra that were carried over several hundred miles by glacier ice.

Drumlins are also distinctive land forms, sometimes known as "baskets of eggs." They are long, low mounds formed from fine clay moraines, packed around scattered boulders. The side facing the direction from which the ice came is steeper than the other side, giving the drumlin its egglike shape. There is a field of 4,000 drumlins in Wisconsin and another of 10,000 in New York State.

▼ These drumlins are clearly defined as they are much more fertile than the land around them.

▶ These erratics in Greenland are different types of rock brought together by glaciers long ago.

14

▲ The scratches, or *striations*, on these rocks were made by glaciers pulling and scraping across them.

Eskers are steep-sided ridges made from the sand and gravel left by rivers that flowed beneath the ice. Eskers are a common feature in the lowlands of Finland. *Kames* are formed when rock waste collects in small lakes on the surface or at the edge of a glacier. After the ice has melted, the kame is left as an oddly shaped mass along the valley floor.

Other signs of glacial movement are the deep scratch marks that show where ice and rock scraped over the ground.

History in the ice

In the mid-18th century, some scientists suggested that Earth had once been covered in ice. They noticed that far below the present glaciers the rocks showed signs of the scratching and smoothing actions of ice. Other people laughed and said the landscape had been shaped by the great flood of Noah's time. In 1836 a scientist named Louis Agassiz set out to contradict the idea that the landscapes of Northwestern Europe had been affected by glaciers, but instead discovered proof that it was true.

▲ Watching you, watching me! Scientific expeditions help us to learn about polar animals such as the emperor penguin.

ice drill

Today, scientists can discover much about the climates of the past. One method is to remove ice from an ice sheet with powerful drills. Scientists in the Antarctic have drilled two holes more than a mile deep. When ice from this great depth has been removed, it is "read" for information. The oxygen in water contains a little radioactivity. This decreases at a fixed rate each year, so by measuring the level of radioactivity in the ice, it is possible to establish its age.

Sometimes there is dust and soil in the ice, which help scientists calculate when Earth was drier than it is today. Air bubbles in the ice contain carbon dioxide, one of the gases people think is contributing to *global warming*, an increase in temperature around the world. Scientists measure the amount of carbon dioxide in the ice to discover its effect in starting and ending ice ages.

▶ Scientists also work below the ice. These divers wear special wet suits to protect them against the extreme cold of these waters. Their breathing equipment allows them to work underwater for long periods.

16

The polar regions

The North and South Poles are surrounded by ice. The Arctic, in the north, is a region of frozen water surrounded by land; the Antarctic, in the south, is land surrounded by sea. These regions are often described as deserts because, like hot deserts, they have very little rainfall. Both regions also have extremely low temperatures, with a short summer of continuous daylight and a very long, cold, dark winter.

▲ These great icebergs are in Antarctica. The smaller icebergs in the front of the picture have calved from the bigger ones.

▶ During the winter the Antarctic is a frozen mass, but as spring and summer approach the ice breaks up. These smaller blocks of floating, frozen saltwater are called *pack ice*. About 7 percent of the world's oceans are covered by pack ice.

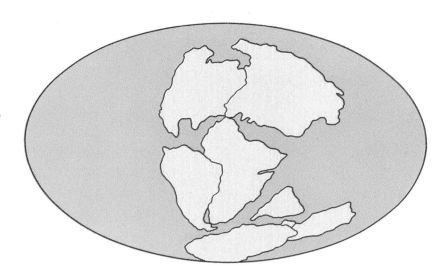

► A map of the world 180 million years ago looks very different from the world today. The giant continent of Gondwanaland was starting to split into a number of smaller continents. Antarctica-Australia and India were breaking away from what would become Africa and South America.

Both polar regions are surrounded by *ice shelves*. An ice shelf is a floating sheet of ice or ice cap anchored to land where the air temperature is always below freezing. The largest is the Ross Ice Shelf in the Antarctic. It holds about one third of the shelf ice in the continent of Antarctica and is about the same size as France. When you approach it from the sea, it towers over you as a 100-foot (30-meter) high cliff.

Icebergs are floating islands of ice that have broken away, or *calved*, from ice shelves. They can be huge. One was seen in the South Atlantic 200 miles (320 kilometers) long and 60 miles (95 kilometers) wide. Only the tip of the iceberg shows above sea level. The rest, which can be as much as seven times as large, is hidden below the surface.

Antarctica has not always been frozen. Scientists think that it was once part of a massive supercontinent, Gondwanaland, which also included the land masses we now call Australia, India, Africa, and South America. Fossils of trees, reptiles, and marsupials have been found in Antarctica. They must have lived there when its climate was warmer.

Explorers of the ice

About 17,000 years ago, the first explorers arrived in the Arctic. They were hunters and trappers, and their descendants still live in the region. They are the Inuit, which in their language means "people." The American Indians used to call them Eskimos, which means "eaters of raw meat." In the 16th century, many Europeans searched for a Northwest Passage through the American continent to the riches of China and India. They never managed to find one, but they did discover the Canadian Arctic.

People had thought for a long time that there must be a southern continent to balance the one in the far north, but the Antarctic was not discovered until Captain James Cook sailed across the Antarctic Circle in 1773. Cook was the first person to see the ice sheets of the Antarctic. He thought the area was totally unsuitable for humans to live in, but he did report that there were big herds of whales and seals living there. Many seal hunters went south and discovered many islands off the Antarctic continent.

▼ This Inuit man is hunting a whale in the traditional manner by throwing a harpoon.

It was not until the end of the 19th century that people realized sailing ships would never reach the North Pole. Fridtjof Nansen set sail for the Arctic in the 1890s. His ship, the *Fram*, had been specially designed to withstand the crushing pressure of the pack ice. Nansen believed that if he deliberately froze his ship into the ice, the underwater currents would make it drift to the North Pole, but he was wrong. Instead he set off for the Pole with a sled and a companion, but they never reached their goal. They did, however, return safely.

▼ Although the *Fram* was specially designed to withstand the force of the ice, it looks very fragile.

One of the great stories of ice exploration is the race between Captain Robert Scott and Roald Amundsen to be the first to reach the South Pole. It was a long, hard journey, and from the start few things went right for Scott. He chose to travel with ponies, which could not stand the cold and died. The men had to drag their own sleds. Amundsen was better equipped and chose a better route. He reached the Pole on December 14, 1911, followed on January 18, 1912 by Scott, who was bitterly disappointed to discover that the Norwegian explorer had beaten him. Amundsen returned safely, but Scott and the rest of his team died on the return journey, only 11 miles (17 kilometers) from their base.

▼ The early polar explorers had to carry everything with them from the beginning of their journey. Today's explorers have their food and medical supplies flown in by aircraft.

▼ Scott and his companions wearily drag their sledges. If they had had husky dogs to do this for them they might have survived. Even today people use huskies because they can cope with the fierce polar weather.

Since these early journeys, many people have traveled to the North and South Poles. Although explorers today can keep in touch by radio with their back-up teams, weather and ice are still great hazards that cannot be ignored. Most present-day explorers are scientists searching for minerals and researching the effects of pollution on our environment.

Plants and animals

The plants and animals that live at the ice caps have developed special ways of surviving the cold. The Antarctic is colder than the Arctic, so there is very little plant or wildlife there. There are a few mosses and lichens that cling to the surface of exposed rocks, but little else. There are no trees in the Arctic, so it is difficult to make fires for cooking. This is probably why the Inuit were called Eskimos, because they could not cook their meat. Lichens and mosses are quite common in the Arctic. These plants are tough, low growers that can survive beneath the snow during the winter months and flower and grow during the summer. Flowering plants grow close to the ground for protection against the winds. Mountain sorrel and mountain buttercup grow at temperatures as low as 23°F (−5°C). Their leaves are specially shaped to use the little sunlight and water.

▲ Cotton grass grows in the rich, moist, marshland soils of the tundra during the short Arctic summer.

◄ This Arctic poppy looks similar to poppies that grow in temperate regions, but it has developed so that it can survive in the rocky tundra region. It grows low so that it can trap the slightly warmer air a few inches above the ground, and its flowers are specially shaped to catch all available sunlight.

24

arctic hare

Between the ice cover around the North Pole and the tree line farther south where the forests begin, there is a huge mass of land called the *tundra*. The tundra is covered by snow for almost nine months of the year. Many plants, animals, and birds have adapted to its harsh conditions. The plants on the tundra provide food for the animals that spend the summer there. Arctic mammals tend to have smaller features, for example ears, than mammals from warmer climates. This is an adaptation to the cold, as smaller features lose heat more slowly than larger ones. The white coats of the polar bear, arctic hare, and arctic fox are another way of keeping heat in the body. Heat is drawn through the white fur to the animal's dark skin. Any heat that is reflected away from the skin is then sent back again by the white fur.

Both the fur and the hooves of Arctic animals are adapted to cope with the cold. Caribou and musk ox have very thick coats with hollow hairs that trap the air and keep the animals warmer. Their large, broad hooves are split to make walking on the snow easier. The hooves also have sharp edges, so the animals can chip through the ice to get at the lichens they eat. Frostbite is never a problem for Arctic animals. The blood going into their hooves passes close to a vein carrying the blood away from them, so that the animal always has cold feet. This means that their feet cannot get colder! Caribou noses are also protected in this way so they can feed without getting a frozen nose.

Large groups of sea birds, such as auks, storm petrels, puffins, and fulmars, are common in the Arctic. They breed there during the spring and migrate to the warmer waters of the Pacific and Atlantic oceans in winter.

▲ A herd of caribou migrate to warmer forest areas to avoid the bitterly cold Arctic winter.

◀ An arctic fox stalks the ground in search of food. Its thick, white coat gives off less heat than a dark one would and helps keep it warm. It also provides good camouflage against the light landscape.

krill

In the Antarctic, penguins live on the ice and in the sea. Their bodies are covered with a thick layer of water-repellent feathers that trap the air to retain heat. All the animals of the Arctic and Antarctic have a thick layer of fat that also protects them against the cold. This is built up every summer to last the winter.

Some types of whales live in the seas around the ice caps of the North and South Poles. They tend to spend the summer in the polar regions, then migrate to warmer waters during the winter. The Antarctic Ocean contains great quantities of *krill*. These are tiny, shrimplike creatures that are the main food supply of seals, whales, birds, and fish. Krill are now being caught for human consumption, and scientists fear this could be disastrous for animal life in the Antarctic.

The future of the ice caps

The Arctic and the Antarctic are probably the largest unspoiled desert areas in the world. They are also the coldest and windiest places. Temperatures in the Antarctic can fall to as low as −127°F (−88°C), and winds howl at up to 65 miles (100 kilometers) per hour. Many countries have set up scientific bases in both polar regions, particularly in the Antarctic. Some scientists study the atmosphere, geology, and wildlife, while others mine the natural resources. Scientists in the Antarctic discovered the hole in the ozone layer that surrounds Earth.

▶ A polar bear and her cub travel across the snow- and ice-covered Hudson Bay in Canada.

▼ Large bases like this bring people—and their waste—to unspoiled areas. The Antarctica Treaty tries to control the amount of scientific work and exploitation of the region.

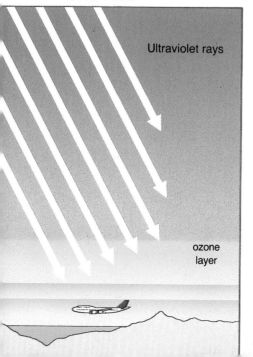

▼ This diagram shows the ozone layer, which lies about 15 to 20 miles (25 to 30 kilometers) above sea level. The ozone layer protects Earth from too many harmful ultraviolet rays from the sun.

Ultraviolet rays

ozone layer

In 1959, 12 countries signed the Antarctica Treaty. This stated that they would work together to find out about and look after the area. By 1990, 37 countries had signed the treaty. Unfortunately, certain things have happened that many people think might destroy this beautiful wilderness forever. Despite the treaty, some countries have begun to develop the area. They have started to mine its rich mineral resources and overfish the seas. In the Arctic, drilling for oil has polluted the environment.

The ice caps and glaciers have been, and still are, essential to Earth's environment. No one is sure whether Earth's temperature will rise or fall in the future. But we know how much climate affects life on our planet.

Fact file

Longest glacier
The longest glacier is the Lambert Glacier in Antarctica. It is at least 250 miles (402 kilometers) long and up to 40 miles (65 kilometers) wide.

Longest valley glacier
The longest valley glacier is the Siachen glacier in Mongolia. It is 47 miles (76 kilometers) long. When the Siachen joins the Hispar and Biafo glaciers, it extends to a total of 76 miles (122 kilometers).

Fastest glacier
The fastest moving glacier is the Quarayaq in Greenland, which moves about 80 feet (24 meters) per day.

Extent of ice caps and glaciers
It is estimated that the ice caps in Antarctica and Greenland contain about 75 percent of the world's fresh water. More than one tenth of Earth's surface is covered by glaciers.

Mount Erebus
Mount Erebus in Antarctica is the most southerly active volcano known in the world. It is 12,448 feet (3,794 meters) high.

Thickest ice
The greatest measured thickness of ice is in Antarctica, where 15,682 feet (4,777 meters) has been recorded. This is greater than the height of most mountains.

▲ The Ross Ice Shelf in Antarctica.

▼ The clear air of the Antarctic means that there are often fantastic optical effects like this "mock sun," or *parhelia*.

Freshwater ice

Although seawater is very salty, sea ice isn't. Sea salt cannot be held within ice crystals. Instead it is held as tiny cells of concentrated salt solution in the ice. This drains away gradually through small vertical channels. Ice that is more than a year old is fresh enough to drink when melted. It has been estimated that the largest icebergs could provide a large city with fresh drinking water for 700 years. Some scientists have suggested towing huge icebergs to drought-ridden areas for irrigation and drinking water.

Tallest iceberg

The tallest iceberg recorded was 550 feet (167 meters) high. It was seen near western Greenland in 1958.

▲ The optical illusion of a mirage in Antarctica.

Transantarctic Mountains

The Transantarctic Mountains form one of the world's greatest mountain ranges. Although submerged beneath the ice for most of their length, they stretch a total distance of 3,000 miles (4,800 kilometers).

History in ice

Ice often holds clues to the weather in both recent times and hundreds of years ago. Samples taken from the core of ice can pinpoint when and where there were major volcanic eruptions, sandstorms, the first deforestation, pollution, and nuclear tests.

Danger

Ice falling from glaciers can be extremely dangerous. In 1962 a fall of ice from the summit glacier on Mount Huascarán in Peru killed 3,000 people. Twelve years later an earthquake caused the mountain to lose more ice, and the avalanche that followed killed 70,000 people. In ski resorts, glaciers that are known to be dangerous are watched carefully. Glaciers should always be treated with caution.

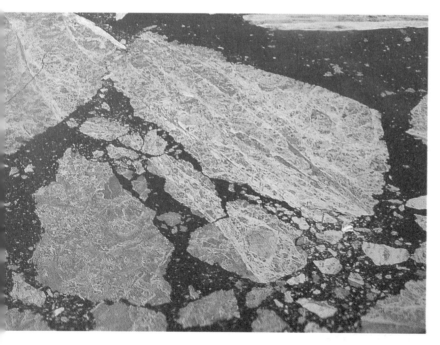

◄ Small floating isles of pancake ice at Baffin Bay in Canada.

31

Index